NEW YORK TEST PREP

Practice Test Book

Common Core Math

Grade 5

ISBN 978-1495210488

CONTENTS

INTRODUCTION
For Parents, Teachers, and Tutors

About the Book

This test book contains two complete New York Mathematics Common Core tests. The tests are just like the tests given by the state of New York. Each test contains the same question types and styles, tests the same skills, and has the same length as the state test. If the student can master the math tests in this book, they will be prepared and ready for the real tests.

Taking the Test

The actual New York math test is divided into three books, as described below. This practice test book also divides each test into three books. To mimic the actual test, students should complete one book each day.

Book	Questions	Suggested Time	Maximum Time Allowed
1	25 multiple-choice questions	40 minutes	80 minutes
2	25 multiple-choice questions	40 minutes	80 minutes
3	6 short-response questions 4 extended-response questions	70 minutes	90 minutes

Recording Answers

For books 1 and 2, students can answer the questions by filling in the circle of their answer choice in the test book. Students can also answer the questions by filling in the circles on the optional answer sheet in the back of the book. For book 3, students should write their answers in the test book.

INTRODUCTION
For Parents, Teachers, and Tutors

Question Types

There are three types of questions found on the state test.

- **Multiple-choice** – students select the correct answer from four options.

- **Short-response** – students provide a brief answer and are usually required to show their work.

- **Extended-response** – students complete a more extensive problem. Students may have to show their work, write an explanation, or justify their answer.

Calculators and Tools

Students are not allowed to use a calculator when taking the actual state test. These tests should be completed without the use of a calculator. Students are given a ruler and protractor to use for all sections of the test. There is also a reference sheet included with each section of the test.

Common Core Math Skills

The math test given by the state of New York covers a specific set of skills and knowledge. These are described in the Common Core Learning Standards (CCLS). These standards were introduced to the New York assessments in 2012-2013, and the state tests are now designed to assess whether students have the skills listed in these standards. Just like the real state tests, the questions in this book cover the skills listed in the CCLS.

The answer key identifies the skill tested by each question, as well as the general topic. Use the topics listed in the answer key to determine areas of strength and weakness. Use the skills listed in the answer key to identify the specific skills and knowledge that the student is lacking. Then target revision and instruction accordingly.

Common Core Mathematics

Grade 5

Practice Test 1

Book 1

Instructions

Read each question carefully. For each multiple-choice question, fill in the circle for the correct answer.

You may use a ruler to help you answer questions.

You may use a protractor to help you answer questions.

Reference Sheet

You may use the information on the Reference Sheet on the next page to help you answer questions.

Grade 5 Mathematics Reference Sheet

Conversions

1 mile = 5,280 feet
1 mile = 1,760 yards

1 pound = 16 ounces
1 ton = 2,000 pounds

1 cup = 8 fluid ounces
1 pint = 2 cups
1 quart = 2 pints
1 gallon = 4 quarts
1 liter = 1,000 cubic centimeters

Formulas

Right Rectangular Prism $V = Bh$ or $V = lwh$

1   To add the fractions below, Wayne first needs to determine the least common multiple of the denominators.

$$\frac{1}{5}, \frac{5}{7}, \frac{9}{10}$$

What is the least common multiple of the denominators?

Ⓐ   35

Ⓑ   50

Ⓒ   70

Ⓓ   350

2   The diagram below shows the length of a piece of ribbon.

$$\frac{12}{100} \text{ meter}$$

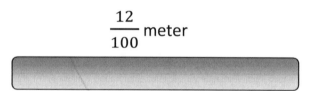

Victoria divides the lace into 4 equal pieces. What is the length of each piece of lace?

Ⓐ $\frac{2}{25}$ meter

Ⓑ $\frac{3}{25}$ meter

Ⓒ $\frac{12}{25}$ meter

Ⓓ $\frac{3}{100}$ meter

3   Donna has $8.45. She spends $3.75. How much money does Donna have left?

   Ⓐ $3.70

   Ⓑ $3.30

   Ⓒ $4.70

   Ⓓ $4.30

4   Hannah cut out a piece of fabric to use for an art project. The length of the fabric was 9.5 yards. The width of the fabric was 3.6 yards less than the length. What was the width of the fabric?

   Ⓐ   5.9 yards

   Ⓑ   6.9 yards

   Ⓒ   12.1 yards

   Ⓓ   13.1 yards

5   Errol is putting photos into albums. Each album has 24 pages for holding photos, and each page can hold 8 photographs. How many photographs could Errol put into 3 photo albums?

   Ⓐ   192

   Ⓑ   376

   Ⓒ   486

   Ⓓ   576

6   Kathy answered $\frac{3}{5}$ of the questions on a test correctly. Which of the following is equivalent to $\frac{3}{5}$?

    Ⓐ   0.3

    Ⓑ   0.35

    Ⓒ   0.6

    Ⓓ   0.65

7   Which ordered pair represents a point located inside both rectangles?

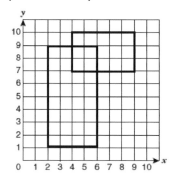

    Ⓐ   (8, 6)

    Ⓑ   (5, 8)

    Ⓒ   (4, 10)

    Ⓓ   (7, 9)

8 To complete a calculation correctly, Mark moves the decimal place of 420.598 two places to the left.

$$420.598 \rightarrow 4.20598$$

Which of these describes the calculation completed?

Ⓐ   Dividing by 10

Ⓑ   Dividing by 100

Ⓒ   Multiplying by 10

Ⓓ   Multiplying by 100

9 Camille cooked a cake on high for $1\frac{1}{4}$ hours. She then cooked it for another $\frac{1}{2}$ hour on low. How long did she cook the cake for in all?

Ⓐ $1\frac{1}{2}$ hours

Ⓑ $1\frac{3}{4}$ hours

Ⓒ $2\frac{1}{4}$ hours

Ⓓ $2\frac{1}{2}$ hours

10   A play sold $222 worth of tickets. Each ticket cost the same amount. Which of these could be the cost of each ticket?

Ⓐ $6

Ⓑ $8

Ⓒ $12

Ⓓ $16

11   A piece of note paper has side lengths of 12.5 centimeters. What is the area of the piece of note paper?

Ⓐ   144.25 square centimeters

Ⓑ   144.5 square centimeters

Ⓒ   156.25 square centimeters

Ⓓ   156.5 square centimeters

12   Cody drew a quadrilateral on a coordinate grid, as shown below.

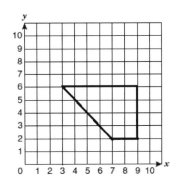

Which of these is NOT the coordinates of one of the vertices of the quadrilateral?

Ⓐ   (7, 2)

Ⓑ   (9, 2)

Ⓒ   (6, 9)

Ⓓ   (3, 6)

13   Sandy has $12.90. Marvin has $18.50. What is the total value of their money?

Ⓐ $3.04

Ⓑ $3.14

Ⓒ $30.40

Ⓓ $31.40

14 The top of a desk is 4 feet long and 3 feet wide. Raymond wants to cover the top of the desk with a vinyl sheet. The vinyl sheet is measured in square inches. What is the area of the vinyl sheet that will cover the top of the desk exactly?

    Ⓐ   12 square inches

    Ⓑ   144 square inches

    Ⓒ   168 square inches

    Ⓓ   1,728 square inches

15 A block is in the shape of a cube. If the side length is represented by x, which of these could be used to find the volume of the cube?

    Ⓐ $3x$

    Ⓑ $6(x^2)$

    Ⓒ $6x$

    Ⓓ x^3

16 Denise made the line plot below to show how long she read for each weekday for 4 weeks.

Daily Reading Time (hours)

How long did Denise read for in total over the 4 weeks?

Ⓐ   8 hours

Ⓑ   9 hours

Ⓒ   10 hours

Ⓓ   11 hours

17   The point below is translated 2 units to the left and 3 units down. What are the coordinates of the point after the translation?

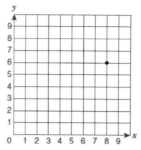

Ⓐ   (6, 3)

Ⓑ   (6, 9)

Ⓒ   (10, 3)

Ⓓ   (10, 9)

18 The table below shows the total number of pounds of flour in different numbers of bags of flour.

Number of Bags	Number of Pounds
3	12
5	20
8	32
9	36

Based on the relationship in the table, how many ounces of flour are in each bag?

Ⓐ   4 ounces

Ⓑ   12 ounces

Ⓒ   64 ounces

Ⓓ   192 ounces

19 The model below is made up of 1-centimeter cubes. What is a correct way to find the volume of the model?

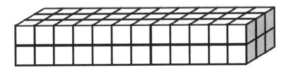

Ⓐ   12 cm x 6 cm

Ⓑ   12 cm x 12 cm

Ⓒ   2 cm x 6 cm x 12 cm

Ⓓ   2 cm x 3 cm x 12 cm

20   Which decimal is plotted on the number line below?

Ⓐ   2.25

Ⓑ   2.3

Ⓒ   2.6

Ⓓ   2.75

21   The wingspan of the butterfly is 6.7 centimeters.

What is the wingspan of the butterfly in millimeters?

Ⓐ   0.067 mm

Ⓑ   0.67 mm

Ⓒ   67 mm

Ⓓ   670 mm

22   Jason used cubes to make the model shown below. What is the volume of the model?

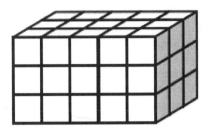

   Ⓐ   15 cubic units

   Ⓑ   45 cubic units

   Ⓒ   50 cubic units

   Ⓓ   75 cubic units

23   The pattern below starts at 0 and uses the rule "Add 4."

0, 4, 8, 12, 16

A second pattern starts at 2 and uses the rule "Add 4." How does the fifth term in the second pattern compare to the fifth term in the first pattern?

   Ⓐ   It is 2 greater.

   Ⓑ   It is 4 greater.

   Ⓒ   It is 8 greater.

   Ⓓ   It is 10 greater.

24   The table below shows a set of number pairs.

x	y
2	−2
3	0
4	2

If the points were plotted on a coordinate grid, which of the following would be the coordinates of one of the points?

Ⓐ   (0, 2)

Ⓑ   (2, 2)

Ⓒ   (4, 2)

Ⓓ   (3, 4)

25   Brian made 16 paper cranes in 15 minutes. If he continues making cranes at this rate, how many cranes would he make in 2 hours?

Ⓐ   32

Ⓑ   64

Ⓒ   120

Ⓓ   128

END OF BOOK 1

Common Core Mathematics

Grade 5

Practice Test 1

Book 2

Instructions

Read each question carefully. For each multiple-choice question, fill in the circle for the correct answer.

You may use a ruler to help you answer questions.

You may use a protractor to help you answer questions.

Reference Sheet

You may use the information on the Reference Sheet on the next page to help you answer questions.

Grade 5 Mathematics Reference Sheet

Conversions

1 mile = 5,280 feet
1 mile = 1,760 yards

1 pound = 16 ounces
1 ton = 2,000 pounds

1 cup = 8 fluid ounces
1 pint = 2 cups
1 quart = 2 pints
1 gallon = 4 quarts
1 liter = 1,000 cubic centimeters

Formulas

Right Rectangular Prism $V = Bh$ or $V = lwh$

26   The model below is made up of 1-centimeter cubes. What is a correct way to find the volume of the cube?

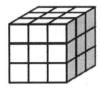

Ⓐ $3 + 3 + 3$

Ⓑ 3^2

Ⓒ 3^3

Ⓓ $6(3^2)$

27   Jason is buying baseball cards. Each packet of baseball cards contains 12 baseball cards and costs $3. How many baseball cards can Jason buy for $15?

Ⓐ   5

Ⓑ   60

Ⓒ   180

Ⓓ   540

28   Which point represents the location of the ordered pair $(1\frac{1}{4}, 2\frac{1}{2})$?

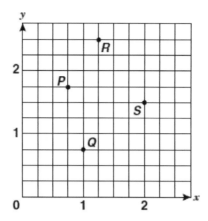

Ⓐ   Point *P*

Ⓑ   Point *Q*

Ⓒ   Point *R*

Ⓓ   Point *S*

29   Which term describes all the shapes shown below?

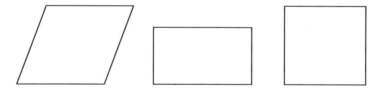

Ⓐ   Parallelogram

Ⓑ   Rectangle

Ⓒ   Rhombus

Ⓓ   Square

30   The table below shows the total cost of hiring DVDs for different numbers of DVDs.

Number of DVDs	Total Cost
2	$6
5	$15
6	$18
8	$24

Which equation could be used to find the total cost, *c*, of hiring *x* DVDs?

Ⓐ $c = x + 4$

Ⓑ $c = 3x$

Ⓒ $c = x + 3$

Ⓓ $c = 8x$

31   Dave bought 4 packets of pies. Three packets had 12 pies each, and one packet had 10 pies. Which number sentence shows the total number of pies Dave bought?

Ⓐ   (3 x 12) x 10

Ⓑ   (3 + 12) x 10

Ⓒ   (3 x 12) + 10

Ⓓ   (3 + 12) + 10

32 Which measurement is equivalent to 3 yards?

    Ⓐ   12 feet

    Ⓑ   36 feet

    Ⓒ   72 inches

    Ⓓ   108 inches

33 The table below shows the cost of hiring items from a hire store.

Item	Cost per Week
CD	$2
DVD	$3
Video game	$4

Which expression represents the total cost of hiring c CDs and d DVDs for w weeks?

    Ⓐ $2c + 3d + w$

    Ⓑ $w(2c + 3d)$

    Ⓒ $w(2c) + 3d$

    Ⓓ $2c + 3d$

34 If the numbers below were each rounded to the nearest tenth, which number would be rounded down?

Ⓐ   17.386

Ⓑ   35.682

Ⓒ   23.758

Ⓓ   76.935

35 The model below was made with 1-unit cubes.

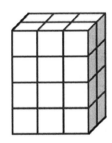

What is the volume of the model?

Ⓐ   12 cubic units

Ⓑ   24 cubic units

Ⓒ   26 cubic units

Ⓓ   36 cubic units

36   The graph below shows a line segment with 3 points marked.

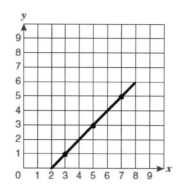

Which table shows the coordinates of these 3 points?

(A)

x	1	2	3
y	3	5	7

(B)

x	3	5	7
y	1	3	5

(C)

x	1	3	5
y	1	2	3

(D)

x	1	3	5
y	3	5	7

37   Joanne had three singing lessons one week. Two lessons went for 45 minutes, and one lesson went for 60 minutes. Which number sentence could be used to find how many minutes Joanne had singing lessons for?

Ⓐ   2 x (45 + 60)

Ⓑ   (45 + 60) ÷ 3

Ⓒ   (2 x 45) + 60

Ⓓ   (2 × 45) + (2 × 60)

38   How is the numeral 9.007 written in words?

Ⓐ   Nine and seven tenths

Ⓑ   Nine and seven thousandths

Ⓒ   Nine and seven hundredths

Ⓓ   Nine thousand and seven

39 The model below shows $1\frac{6}{100}$ shaded.

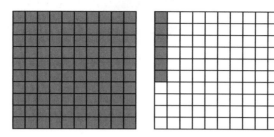

What decimal represents the shaded part of the model?

Ⓐ   1.6

Ⓑ   1.06

Ⓒ   0.16

Ⓓ   0.106

40 A rectangular toy box has a length of 90 centimeters, a width of 30 centimeters, and a height of 50 centimeters. What is the volume of the toy box?

Ⓐ   4,500 cubic centimeters

Ⓑ   6,000 cubic centimeters

Ⓒ   81,000 cubic centimeters

Ⓓ   135,000 cubic centimeters

41 A glass of water had a temperature of 25°C. Derek heated the water so that the temperature increased by 3°C every 10 minutes. What would the temperature of the water have been after 30 minutes?

Ⓐ   28°C

Ⓑ   31°C

Ⓒ   34°C

Ⓓ   37°C

42 Mr. Singh bought 2 adult zoo tickets for a total of $22, as well as 4 children's tickets. He spent $54 in total. How much was each children's ticket?

Ⓐ $8

Ⓑ $2.50

Ⓒ $9

Ⓓ $13.50

43 Emily cooked a roast on high for $1\frac{1}{2}$ hours. She then cooked it for another $1\frac{3}{4}$ hour on low. How long did she cook the roast for in all?

Ⓐ $2\frac{1}{4}$ hours

Ⓑ $2\frac{3}{4}$ hours

Ⓒ $3\frac{1}{4}$ hours

Ⓓ $3\frac{3}{4}$ hours

44   Which operation in the expression should be carried out first?

$$42 + 24 \div (3 - 1) + 5$$

Ⓐ   42 + 24

Ⓑ   24 ÷ 3

Ⓒ   3 − 1

Ⓓ   3 + 5

45   Leanne added $\frac{1}{4}$ cup of milk and $\frac{3}{8}$ cup of water to a bowl. Which diagram is shaded to show how many cups of milk and water were in the bowl in all?

Ⓐ

Ⓑ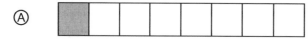

Ⓒ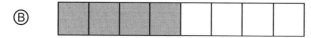

Ⓓ

46 The cost of renting a trailer is a basic fee of $20 plus an additional $25 for each day that the trailer is rented.

Which equation can be used to find *c*, the cost in dollars of the rental for *d* days?

Ⓐ $c = 20d + 25$

Ⓑ $c = 25d + 20$

Ⓒ $c = 20(d + 25)$

Ⓓ $c = 25(d + 20)$

47 Which two shapes have the same number of sides?

Ⓐ   Triangle and rectangle

Ⓑ   Rectangle and square

Ⓒ   Hexagon and pentagon

Ⓓ   Pentagon and triangle

48   A bulldog weighs 768 ounces. How many pounds does the bulldog weigh?

   Ⓐ   48 pounds

   Ⓑ   64 pounds

   Ⓒ   96 pounds

   Ⓓ   192 pounds

49   A square garden has side lengths of $4\frac{1}{2}$ feet. What is the area of the garden? You can use the diagram below to help find the answer.

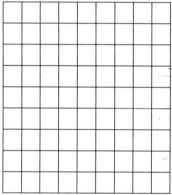

Each square is $\frac{1}{2}$ foot × $\frac{1}{2}$ foot.

Each square has an area of $\frac{1}{4}$ square feet.

   Ⓐ $16\frac{1}{4}$ square feet

   Ⓑ $20\frac{1}{4}$ square feet

   Ⓒ $40\frac{1}{2}$ square feet

   Ⓓ $182\frac{1}{4}$ square feet

50   Maxwell bought a packet of 48 baseball cards. He gave 8 baseball cards to each of 4 friends. Which number sentence can be used to find the number of baseball cards Maxwell has left?

Ⓐ $(48 - 8) \times 4$

Ⓑ $(48 - 8) \div 4$

Ⓒ $48 - (8 + 4)$

Ⓓ $48 - (8 \times 4)$

END OF BOOK 2

Common Core Mathematics

Grade 5

Practice Test 1

Book 3

Instructions

Read each question carefully. For each multiple-choice question, fill in the circle for the correct answer.

You may use a ruler to help you answer questions.

You may use a protractor to help you answer questions.

Reference Sheet

You may use the information on the Reference Sheet on the next page to help you answer questions.

Grade 5 Mathematics Reference Sheet

Conversions

1 mile = 5,280 feet
1 mile = 1,760 yards

1 pound = 16 ounces
1 ton = 2,000 pounds

1 cup = 8 fluid ounces
1 pint = 2 cups
1 quart = 2 pints
1 gallon = 4 quarts
1 liter = 1,000 cubic centimeters

Formulas

Right Rectangular Prism $V = Bh$ or $V = lwh$

51   A school has 7 school buses. Each bus can seat 48 students. A total of 303 students get on the buses to go to a school camp. How many empty seats would there be on the buses?

Show your work.

Answer _____

52   What is the value of the expression below?

$$(16 + 20) - 8 \div 4$$

Show your work.

Answer _____

53 A jug of milk contains 3 quarts of milk. Michael pours 1 pint of milk from the jug. How many pints of milk are left in the jug?

Show your work.

Answer _____ pints

54 A talent contest will go for 100 minutes. The contest is divided into 16 equal segments. How long will each segment go for? You can use the hundreds grid below to help you find your answer.

Show your work.

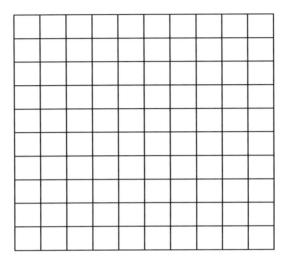

Answer _____ minutes

55   Mike went on vacation to Ohio. When he left home, the odometer read 7,219.4 miles. When he returned home, the odometer read 8,192.6 miles. How many miles did Mike travel?

Show your work.

Answer _____ miles

56   The table below shows the prices of items at a cake stall.

Item	Price
Small cake	$1.85
Muffin	$2.25
Cookie	$0.95

Frankie bought a small cake and a cookie. Bronwyn bought a muffin. How much more did Frankie spend than Bronwyn?

Show your work.

Answer _____

57   The grid below represents Dani's living room.

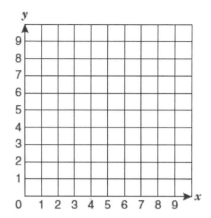

The television is located at the point (5, 4). A lamp is sitting 4 units to the right of the television and 3 units down from the television. What ordered pair represents the location of the lamp?

Answer _____

Explain how you found your answer.

_____

_____

_____

_____

58 The list below shows data a science class collected on the diameter of hailstones that fell during a storm.

Hailstone Diameter (inches)

$$\frac{1}{4}, \frac{1}{4}, \frac{1}{2}, \frac{5}{8}, \frac{1}{2}, \frac{3}{8}, \frac{5}{8}, \frac{1}{4}, \frac{7}{8}, \frac{3}{4}$$

Part A

Plot the data on the line plot below.

Hailstone Diameter (inches)

| 0 | $\frac{1}{8}$ | $\frac{1}{4}$ | $\frac{3}{8}$ | $\frac{1}{2}$ | $\frac{5}{8}$ | $\frac{3}{4}$ | $\frac{7}{8}$ | 1 |

Part B

The median is the middle value when the diameters are placed in order. Use the line plot you made to find the median diameter.

Answer _____ inch

Explain how you used the line plot to find your answer.

_____

_____

_____

_____

59   Tom worked for 32 hours and earned $448. He earned the same rate per hour.

Part A

Write an equation that can be solved to find how much Tom earns per hour. Use *h* to represent how much Tom earns per hour.

Equation _____

Part B

Solve the equation to find much Tom earns per hour.

Show your work.

Answer _____

60   Mitch ran 2.6 miles on Monday and 1.8 miles on Tuesday. How many miles less did Mitch run on Tuesday? Use the diagram below to find the answer.

Answer _____ miles

Explain how you used the diagram to find your answer.

_____

_____

_____

_____

END OF BOOK 3

Common Core Mathematics

Grade 5

Practice Test 2

Book 1

Instructions

Read each question carefully. For each multiple-choice question, fill in the circle for the correct answer.

You may use a ruler to help you answer questions.

You may use a protractor to help you answer questions.

Reference Sheet

You may use the information on the Reference Sheet on the next page to help you answer questions.

Grade 5 Mathematics Reference Sheet

Conversions

1 mile = 5,280 feet
1 mile = 1,760 yards

1 pound = 16 ounces
1 ton = 2,000 pounds

1 cup = 8 fluid ounces
1 pint = 2 cups
1 quart = 2 pints
1 gallon = 4 quarts
1 liter = 1,000 cubic centimeters

Formulas

Right Rectangular Prism $\qquad$ $V = Bh$ or $V = lwh$

1   The decimal cards for 0.59 and 0.22 are shown below.

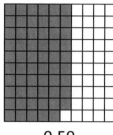   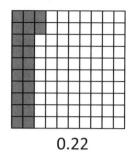

    0.59   0.22

What is the difference of 0.59 and 0.22?

Ⓐ   0.39

Ⓑ   0.37

Ⓒ   0.81

Ⓓ   0.83

2   Joy made 24 apple pies for a bake sale. Each serving was $\frac{1}{8}$ of a pie. How many servings did Joy make?

Ⓐ   3

Ⓑ   32

Ⓒ   96

Ⓓ   192

3   Look at the fractions below.

$$1\frac{1}{3},\ 2\frac{1}{2},\ 3\frac{5}{6}$$

Which procedure can be used to find the sum of the fractions?

Ⓐ   Find the sum of the whole numbers, find the sum of the fractions, and then add the two sums

Ⓑ   Find the sum of the whole numbers, find the sum of the fractions, and then multiply the two sums

Ⓒ   Find the sum of the whole numbers, find the sum of the fractions, and then subtract the two sums

Ⓓ   Find the sum of the whole numbers, find the sum of the fractions, and then divide the two sums

4   Which shape represented below does NOT always have at least one pair of congruent sides?

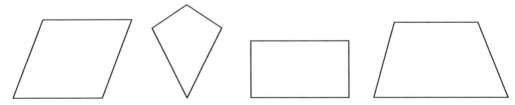

Ⓐ   Rectangle

Ⓑ   Rhombus

Ⓒ   Trapezoid

Ⓓ   Kite

5 A diner has 18 tables. Each table can seat 4 people. The diner also has 8 benches that can each seat 6 people. How many people can the diner seat in all?

Ⓐ   36

Ⓑ   120

Ⓒ   260

Ⓓ   308

6 A fraction representing $\frac{6}{8}$ is shown below.

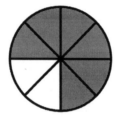

What is the value of $\frac{6}{8} \div 3$?

Ⓐ $\frac{1}{8}$

Ⓑ $\frac{3}{8}$

Ⓒ $\frac{1}{4}$

Ⓓ $\frac{3}{4}$

7   What is the value of the expression below?

$$42 + 24 \div 3 + 3$$

Ⓐ   22

Ⓑ   25

Ⓒ   46

Ⓓ   53

8   Keegan's family drinks about 2 gallons of milk every 5 days.

About how many quarts of milk does Keegan's family drink in 30 days?

Ⓐ   24 quarts

Ⓑ   48 quarts

Ⓒ   240 quarts

Ⓓ   300 quarts

9 Chan spent $\frac{3}{8}$ of his total homework time completing his science homework. What calculation could be used to convert the fraction to a decimal?

Ⓐ $3 \div 8 \times 100$

Ⓑ $8 \div 3 \times 100$

Ⓒ $3 \div 8$

Ⓓ $8 \div 3$

10 A recipe for pancakes requires $2\frac{2}{3}$ cups of flour. Donna only has $1\frac{1}{2}$ cups of flour. How many more cups of flour does Donna need?

Ⓐ $\frac{1}{3}$ cup

Ⓑ $\frac{1}{6}$ cup

Ⓒ $1\frac{1}{3}$ cups

Ⓓ $1\frac{1}{6}$ cups

11 There are 6 reams of paper in a box. There are 144 boxes of paper on a pallet. How many reams of paper are on a pallet?

Ⓐ   24

Ⓑ   576

Ⓒ   644

Ⓓ   864

12 Byron made 9 baskets out of 15 baskets he attempted. What fraction of his baskets did he make?

Ⓐ $\dfrac{1}{3}$

Ⓑ $\dfrac{1}{6}$

Ⓒ $\dfrac{3}{5}$

Ⓓ $\dfrac{3}{10}$

13 The mass of a car is 1.56 tons. What is the mass of the car in pounds?

Ⓐ   312 pounds

Ⓑ   3,120 pounds

Ⓒ   31,200 pounds

Ⓓ   312,000 pounds

14   The table below shows a set of number pairs.

x	y
1	1
3	5
5	9

Which equation shows the relationship between x and y?

Ⓐ $y = x + 2$

Ⓑ $y = x + 4$

Ⓒ $y = 2x - 1$

Ⓓ $y = 3x - 4$

15   Leonard bought 12 tickets to a charity event. The total cost of the tickets was $216. The expression below can be used to find the cost of each ticket.

$$216 \div 12$$

Which of the following is equivalent to the above expression?

Ⓐ $(240 \div 12) + (24 \div 12)$

Ⓑ $(200 \div 10) + (16 \div 2)$

Ⓒ $(216 \div 10) + (216 \div 2)$

Ⓓ $(120 \div 12) + (96 \div 12)$

16   Which term does NOT describe the figure below?

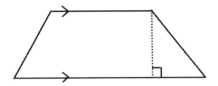

   Ⓐ   Parallelogram

   Ⓑ   Polygon

   Ⓒ   Quadrilateral

   Ⓓ   Trapezoid

17   Which point is located at (6, 3)?

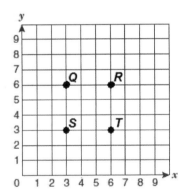

   Ⓐ   Point *Q*

   Ⓑ   Point *R*

   Ⓒ   Point *S*

   Ⓓ   Point *T*

18 The table below shows the relationship between the original price and the sale price of a book.

Original price, P	Sale price, S
$10	$7.50
$12	$9
$14	$10.50
$16	$12

What is the rule to find the sale price of a book, in dollars?

Ⓐ $S = 0.25P$

Ⓑ $S = 0.75P$

Ⓒ $S = P - 2.5$

Ⓓ $S = P - 7.5$

19 Leo measures the length, width, and height of a block. He multiplies the length, width, and height. What is Leo finding?

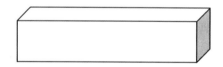

Ⓐ   Surface area

Ⓑ   Mass

Ⓒ   Volume

Ⓓ   Perimeter

20   Which figure below does NOT have any parallel sides?

Ⓐ

Ⓑ

Ⓒ

Ⓓ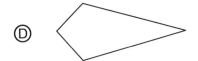

21   If $p = 5$, what is the value of $4(p + 7)$?

Ⓐ   16

Ⓑ   27

Ⓒ   48

Ⓓ   64

22   The cost of renting a windsurfer is a basic fee of $15 plus an additional $5 for each hour that the windsurfer is rented. Which equation can be used to find c, the cost in dollars of the rental for h hours?

Ⓐ $c = 15h + 5$

Ⓑ $c = 5h + 15$

Ⓒ $c = 15(h + 5)$

Ⓓ $c = 5(h + 15)$

23   The graph below shows the line segment PQ. Point P is at $(3, 9)$. Point Q is at $(3, 1)$.

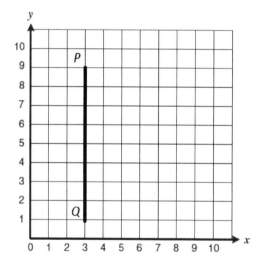

What is the length of the line segment PQ?

Ⓐ   6 units

Ⓑ   8 units

Ⓒ   9 units

Ⓓ   10 units

24 What decimal is equivalent to the fraction $\frac{33}{100}$?

Ⓐ 0.033

Ⓑ 0.33

Ⓒ 33.0

Ⓓ 3.3

25 Which decimal is represented below?

$$(4 \times 100) + (8 \times 1) + (6 \times \frac{1}{100}) + (3 \times \frac{1}{1000})$$

Ⓐ 480.63

Ⓑ 480.063

Ⓒ 408.63

Ⓓ 408.063

END OF BOOK 1

Common Core Mathematics

Grade 5

Practice Test 2

Book 2

Instructions

Read each question carefully. For each multiple-choice question, fill in the circle for the correct answer.

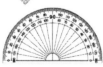

You may use a ruler to help you answer questions.

You may use a protractor to help you answer questions.

Reference Sheet

You may use the information on the Reference Sheet on the next page to help you answer questions.

Grade 5 Mathematics Reference Sheet

Conversions

1 mile = 5,280 feet
1 mile = 1,760 yards

1 pound = 16 ounces
1 ton = 2,000 pounds

1 cup = 8 fluid ounces
1 pint = 2 cups
1 quart = 2 pints
1 gallon = 4 quarts
1 liter = 1,000 cubic centimeters

Formulas

Right Rectangular Prism $V = Bh$ or $V = lwh$

26   Liam drew a triangle with no equal side lengths, as shown below.

What type of triangle did Liam draw?

Ⓐ   Scalene

Ⓑ   Equilateral

Ⓒ   Isosceles

Ⓓ   Right

27   The table below shows the total number of lemons in different numbers of bags of lemons.

Number of Bags	Number of Lemons
2	16
3	24
5	40
8	64

What is the relationship between the number of bags of lemons and the total number of lemons?

Ⓐ   The number of bags is 8 times the number of lemons.

Ⓑ   The number of bags is 16 times the number of lemons.

Ⓒ   The number of lemons is 8 times the number of bags.

Ⓓ   The number of lemons is 16 times the number of bags.

28 Amy ordered 3 pizzas for $6.95 each. She also bought a soft drink for $1.95. Which equation can be used to find how much change, *c*, she should receive from $30?

Ⓐ $c = 30 - 3(6.95 + 1.95)$

Ⓑ $c = 30 - 3(6.95 - 1.95)$

Ⓒ $c = 30 - 6.95 - 1.95$

Ⓓ $c = 30 - (6.95 \times 3) - 1.95$

29 What is the decimal 55.146 rounded to the nearest tenth?

Ⓐ 55.1

Ⓑ 55.2

Ⓒ 55.14

Ⓓ 55.15

30 What is the value of the expression below?

$$28 + 4 \div 2 + (9 - 5)$$

Ⓐ 20

Ⓑ 30

Ⓒ 34

Ⓓ 44

31 The table shows the side length of a rhombus and the perimeter of a rhombus.

Side Length, x (cm)	Perimeter, y (cm)
1	4
2	8
3	12
4	16

Which equation represents the relationship between side length and perimeter?

Ⓐ $y = x + 3$

Ⓑ $y = 4x$

Ⓒ $x = y + 4$

Ⓓ $x = 4y$

32 A florist sells balloons in sets of 6. A customer ordered several sets of 6 balloons. Which of these could be the total number of balloons ordered?

Ⓐ   48

Ⓑ   50

Ⓒ   52

Ⓓ   56

33 The table below shows the amount Davis spent on phone calls for four different months.

Month	Amount
April	$9.22
May	$9.09
June	$9.18
July	$9.05

In which month did David spend the least on phone calls?

Ⓐ   April

Ⓑ   May

Ⓒ   June

Ⓓ   July

34 It took James and his family $2\frac{1}{4}$ hours to drive from their house to the beach. How many minutes did the drive take?

Ⓐ   175 minutes

Ⓑ   75 minutes

Ⓒ   120 minutes

Ⓓ   135 minutes

35   What is the rule to find the value of a term in the sequence below?

Position, n	Value of Term
1	3
2	5
3	7
4	9

Ⓐ $4n - 4$

Ⓑ $3n$

Ⓒ $2n + 1$

Ⓓ $n + 2$

36   The table shows the amount of rainfall for the first four days of May.

Date	1st	2nd	3rd	4th
Rainfall (cm)	4.59	4.43	4.50	4.61

Which day had the lowest rainfall?

Ⓐ   1st

Ⓑ   2nd

Ⓒ   3rd

Ⓓ   4th

37 What value for *x* makes the equation below true?

$$54 \div x = 9$$

Ⓐ 6

Ⓑ 7

Ⓒ 8

Ⓓ 9

38 The grid below represents 4 x 7.

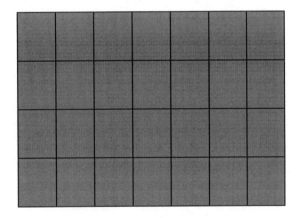

Which of these is another way to represent 4 x 7?

Ⓐ 7 + 7 + 7 + 7

Ⓑ 7 + 7 + 7 + 7 + 7 + 7 + 7

Ⓒ 4 + 4 + 4 + 4

Ⓓ 4 x 4 x 4 x 4

39 Sandy has 129 dimes. Marvin has 185 dimes. What is the total value of Sandy and Marvin's dimes?

Ⓐ $3.04

Ⓑ $3.14

Ⓒ $30.40

Ⓓ $31.40

40 Which of the following is a correct definition of a square?

Ⓐ   A rectangle with two pairs of parallel sides

Ⓑ   A rectangle with adjacent sides perpendicular

Ⓒ   A rhombus with four equal sides

Ⓓ   A rhombus with four right angles

41 Ellen multiplies the number 3 by a fraction. The result is a number greater than 3. Which of these could be the fraction?

Ⓐ $1\frac{1}{4}$

Ⓑ $\frac{8}{9}$

Ⓒ $\frac{1}{6}$

Ⓓ $\frac{1}{2}$

42   Look at the two sequences of numbers below.

First sequence: 0, 4, 8, 12, 16, 20, 24, ...
Second sequence: 0, 8, 16, 24, 32, 40, 48, ...

If the 100th term in the first sequence is represented as n, which of these gives the 100th term in the second sequence?

Ⓐ $n + 4$

Ⓑ $n + 8$

Ⓒ $2n$

Ⓓ $2n + 4$

43   Lloyd bought 4 T-shirts. Each T-shirt cost $7. Which is one way to work out how much change Lloyd would receive from $30?

Ⓐ   Add 4 to 7 and subtract the result from 30

Ⓑ   Add 4 to 7 and add the result to 30

Ⓒ   Multiply 4 by 7 and add the result to 30

Ⓓ   Multiply 4 by 7 and subtract the result from 30

44   An Italian restaurant sells four types of meals. The owner made this table to show how many meals of each type were sold one night. According to the table, which statement is true?

Meal	Number Sold
Pasta	16
Pizza	18
Salad	11
Risotto	9

Ⓐ   The store sold more pizza meals than salad and risotto meals combined.

Ⓑ   The store sold twice as many pizza meals as risotto meals.

Ⓒ   The store sold more pasta meals than any other type of meal.

Ⓓ   The store sold half as many salad meals as pasta meals.

45   Jordan is putting CDs in a case. She can fit 24 CDs in each row. She has 120 CDs. Which equation can be used to find the total number of rows, r, she can fill?

Ⓐ $r \times 120 = 24$

Ⓑ $r \div 24 = 120$

Ⓒ $120 \times 24 = r$

Ⓓ $120 \div 24 = r$

46   Jay made 8 trays of 6 muffins each.

He gave 12 muffins away. He packed the remaining muffins in bags of 4 muffins each. Which expression can be used to find how many bags of muffins he packed?

Ⓐ $(8 \times 6) - 12 \div 4$

Ⓑ $(8 \times 6) - (12 \div 4)$

Ⓒ $8 \times (6 - 12 \div 4)$

Ⓓ $(8 \times 6 - 12) \div 4$

47   The table shows the side length of an equilateral triangle and the perimeter of an equilateral triangle.

Side Length, *l* (inches)	Perimeter, *P* (inches)
2	6
3	9
4	12
5	15

Which equation represents the relationship between side length and perimeter?

Ⓐ $P = l + 4$

Ⓑ $P = 3l$

Ⓒ $l = P + 4$

Ⓓ $l = 3P$

48   Which word best describes the shape of the triangle below?

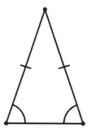

   Ⓐ   Isosceles

   Ⓑ   Scalene

   Ⓒ   Equilateral

   Ⓓ   Right

49   Which of these is equal to 600,000?

   Ⓐ   60 thousands

   Ⓑ   60 ten-thousands

   Ⓒ   60 hundred-thousands

   Ⓓ   60 millions

50   Which statement is true about the product of $\frac{1}{3}$ and 6?

   Ⓐ   The product is greater than 6.

   Ⓑ   The product is less than $\frac{1}{3}$.

   Ⓒ   The product is a value between the two factors.

   Ⓓ   The product is a value equal to one of the factors.

END OF BOOK 2

Common Core Mathematics

Grade 5

Practice Test 2

Book 3

Instructions

Read each question carefully. For each multiple-choice question, fill in the circle for the correct answer.

You may use a ruler to help you answer questions.

You may use a protractor to help you answer questions.

Reference Sheet

You may use the information on the Reference Sheet on the next page to help you answer questions.

Grade 5 Mathematics Reference Sheet

Conversions

1 mile = 5,280 feet
1 mile = 1,760 yards

1 pound = 16 ounces
1 ton = 2,000 pounds

1 cup = 8 fluid ounces
1 pint = 2 cups
1 quart = 2 pints
1 gallon = 4 quarts
1 liter = 1,000 cubic centimeters

Formulas

Right Rectangular Prism $V = Bh$ or $V = lwh$

51 An orchard has a total of 192 orange trees. They are planted in rows of 12 orange trees each. How many rows of orange trees does the orchard have?

Show your work.

Answer _____

52   Joshua bought a pair of sunglasses for $14.85 and a phone case for $2.55. How much change should he receive from $20?

Show your work.

Answer _____

53   The graph below shows a line segment with 3 points marked.

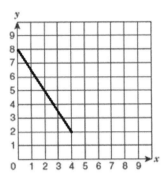

Part A

Complete the table below to show the coordinates of 3 points the line passes through.

x	0	2	4
y			

Part B

What are the coordinates of the point where the line intercepts the y-axis?

Answer _____

54   The model below was made with 1-inch cubes.

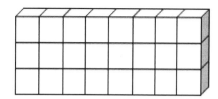

What is the volume of the model? Be sure to include the correct units in your answer.

Show your work.

Answer _____

55 Candice has a painting canvas that is $\frac{3}{4}$ foot long and $\frac{3}{4}$ foot wide. What is the area of the canvas? Shade the diagram below to find the area of the canvas.

Show your work.

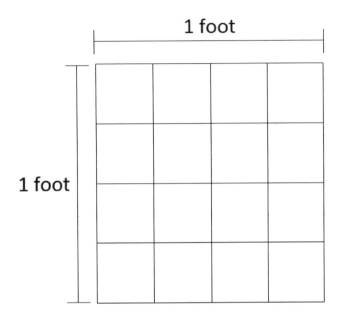

Answer _____ square feet

56 Jasper painted $\frac{1}{2}$ of his room on Saturday. On Sunday, he painted $\frac{1}{3}$ of the remaining part of his room. What fraction of his room does Jasper have left to paint?

Show your work.

Answer _____

57 The grid below represents Roberto's backyard.

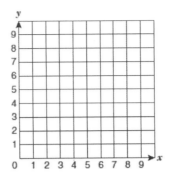

A lemon tree is located at the point (6, 5). An orange tree is located 2 units to the right and 3 units up from the lemon tree. Find the coordinates that represent the location of the orange tree.

Answer _____

Explain how you found your answer.

_____

_____

_____

_____

58   Look at the figure below.

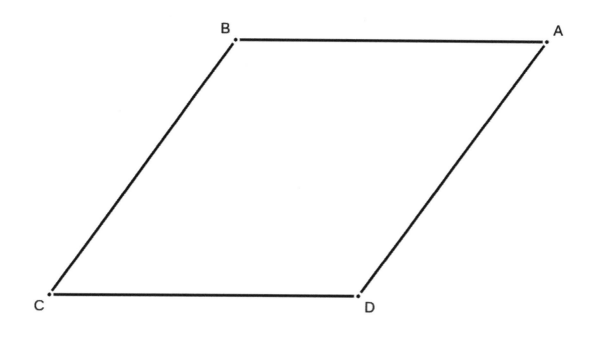

Part A

Identify the two pairs of parallel line segments. Write each line segment on one of the lines below.

Answer _____ and _____, _____ and _____

Part B

Name the shape and describe the properties you used to identify it.

_____

_____

_____

_____

59   The statements below describe quadrilaterals.

At least 1 pair of parallel sides

2 pairs of perpendicular sides

4 equal angles

4 right angles

4 congruent sides

Part A

Circle the statement that correctly describes a trapezoid.

Part B

Which statement above could be used to tell the difference between a rectangle and a square? Explain your answer.

_____

_____

_____

_____

_____

60 A restaurant manager kept a record of the pieces of pie sold one week. He made this list to show the results.

- $\frac{1}{4}$ of the pieces sold were apple pie
- $\frac{3}{8}$ of the pieces sold were pumpkin pie
- $\frac{1}{12}$ of the pieces sold were cherry pie
- The rest of the pieces sold were peach pie.

Part A

What fraction of the pieces sold were peach pie?

Show your work.

Answer _____

Part B

If there were a total of 360 pieces of pie sold that week, how many pieces of cherry pie were sold?

Show your work.

Answer _____

END OF BOOK 3

ANSWER KEY AND SKILLS LIST

Common Core Math Skills

The math test given by the state of New York covers a specific set of skills and knowledge. These are described in the Common Core Learning Standards (CCLS). These standards were introduced to the New York assessments in 2012-2013, and the state tests are now designed to assess whether students have the skills listed in these standards. Just like the real state tests, the questions in this book cover the skills listed in the CCLS.

Assessing Skills and Knowledge

The skills listed in the Common Core Learning Standards are divided into five topics, or clusters. These are:

- Operations and Algebraic Thinking
- Number and Operations in Base Ten
- Number and Operations – Fractions
- Measurement and Data
- Geometry

The answer key identifies the topic for each question. Use the topics listed to identify general areas of strength and weakness. Then target revision and instruction accordingly.

The answer key also identifies the specific math skill that each question is testing. Use the skills listed to identify skills that the student is lacking. Then target revision and instruction accordingly.

Common Core Mathematics, Practice Test 1, Book 1

Question	Answer	Topic	Common Core Skill
1	C	Number & Operations-Fractions	Add and subtract fractions with unlike denominators (including mixed numbers) by replacing given fractions with equivalent fractions in such a way as to produce an equivalent sum or difference of fractions with like denominators.
2	D	Number & Operations-Fractions	Solve real world problems involving division of fractions by whole numbers, e.g., by using visual fraction models and equations to represent the problem.
3	C	Number & Operations in Base Ten	Add, subtract, multiply, and divide decimals to hundredths.
4	A	Number & Operations in Base Ten	Add, subtract, multiply, and divide decimals to hundredths.
5	D	Number & Operations in Base Ten	Fluently multiply multi-digit whole numbers using the standard algorithm.
6	C	Number & Operations-Fractions	Interpret a fraction as division of the numerator by the denominator.
7	B	Geometry	Locate a point in a coordinate system by using an ordered pair of numbers, called its coordinates.
8	B	Number & Operations in Base Ten	Explain patterns in the placement of the decimal point when a decimal is multiplied or divided by a power of 10.
9	B	Number & Operations-Fractions	Add and subtract fractions with unlike denominators (including mixed numbers) by replacing given fractions with equivalent fractions in such a way as to produce an equivalent sum or difference of fractions with like denominators.
10	A	Number & Operations in Base Ten	Find whole-number quotients of whole numbers with up to four-digit dividends and two-digit divisors, using strategies based on place value, the properties of operations, and/or the relationship between multiplication and division.
11	C	Number & Operations in Base Ten	Add, subtract, multiply, and divide decimals to hundredths.
12	C	Geometry	Locate a point in a coordinate system by using an ordered pair of numbers, called its coordinates.
13	D	Number & Operations in Base Ten	Add, subtract, multiply, and divide decimals to hundredths.
14	D	Measurement & Data	Convert among different-sized standard measurement units within a given measurement system, and use these conversions in solving multi-step, real world problems.
15	D	Measurement & Data	Recognize volume as an attribute of solid figures and understand concepts of volume measurement.
16	C	Measurement & Data	Make a line plot to display a data set of measurements in fractions of a unit (1/2, 1/4, 1/8). Use operations on fractions for this grade to solve problems involving information presented in line plots.

17	A	Geometry	Use a coordinate system and understand that the first number indicates how far to travel from the origin in the direction of one axis, and the second number indicates how far to travel in the direction of the second axis.
18	C	Measurement & Data	Convert among different-sized standard measurement units within a given measurement system, and use these conversions in solving multi-step, real world problems.
19	D	Measurement & Data	Relate volume to the operations of multiplication and addition and solve real world and mathematical problems involving volume.
20	C	Number & Operations in Base Ten	Read and write decimals to thousandths using base-ten numerals, number names, and expanded form.
21	C	Measurement & Data	Convert among different-sized standard measurement units within a given measurement system, and use these conversions in solving multi-step, real world problems.
22	B	Measurement & Data	Measure volumes by counting unit cubes, using cubic cm, cubic in, cubic ft, and improvised units.
23	A	Operations/Algebraic Thinking	Generate two numerical patterns using two given rules. Identify apparent relationships between corresponding terms.
24	C	Operations/Algebraic Thinking	Form ordered pairs consisting of corresponding terms from the two patterns, and graph the ordered pairs on a coordinate plane.
25	D	Measurement & Data	Convert among different-sized standard measurement units within a given measurement system, and use these conversions in solving multi-step, real world problems.

Common Core Mathematics, Practice Test 1, Book 2

Question	Answer	Topic	Common Core Skill
26	C	Measurement & Data	Relate volume to the operations of multiplication and addition and solve real world and mathematical problems involving volume.
27	B	Number & Operations in Base Ten	Perform operations with multi-digit whole numbers.
28	C	Geometry	Locate a point in a coordinate system by using an ordered pair of numbers, called its coordinates.
29	A	Geometry	Classify two-dimensional figures in a hierarchy based on properties.
30	B	Operations/Algebraic Thinking	Analyze patterns and relationships by identifying apparent relationships between corresponding terms.
31	C	Operations/Algebraic Thinking	Write simple expressions that record calculations with numbers, and interpret numerical expressions without evaluating them.
32	D	Measurement & Data	Convert among different-sized standard measurement units within a given measurement system, and use these conversions in solving multi-step, real world problems.
33	B	Operations/Algebraic Thinking	Use parentheses, brackets, or braces in numerical expressions, and evaluate expressions with these symbols.
34	D	Number & Operations in Base Ten	Use place value understanding to round decimals to any place.
35	B	Measurement & Data	Measure volumes by counting unit cubes, using cubic cm, cubic in, cubic ft, and improvised units.
36	B	Operations/Algebraic Thinking	Form ordered pairs consisting of corresponding terms from the two patterns, and graph the ordered pairs on a coordinate plane.
37	C	Operations/Algebraic Thinking	Write simple expressions that record calculations with numbers, and interpret numerical expressions without evaluating them.
38	B	Number & Operations in Base Ten	Read and write decimals to thousandths using base-ten numerals, number names, and expanded form.
39	B	Number & Operations in Base Ten	Explain patterns in the placement of the decimal point when a decimal is multiplied or divided by a power of 10.
40	D	Measurement & Data	Apply the formulas $V = l \times w \times h$ and $V = b \times h$ for rectangular prisms to find volumes of right rectangular prisms with whole-number edge lengths in the context of solving real world and mathematical problems.
41	C	Operations/Algebraic Thinking	Analyze patterns and relationships.
42	A	Number & Operations in Base Ten	Perform operations with multi-digit whole numbers.

43	C	Number & Operations-Fractions	Add and subtract fractions with unlike denominators (including mixed numbers) by replacing given fractions with equivalent fractions in such a way as to produce an equivalent sum or difference of fractions with like denominators.
44	C	Operations/Algebraic Thinking	Use parentheses, brackets, or braces in numerical expressions, and evaluate expressions with these symbols.
45	C	Number & Operations-Fractions	Solve word problems involving addition and subtraction of fractions referring to the same whole, including cases of unlike denominators, e.g., by using visual fraction models or equations to represent the problem.
46	B	Operations/Algebraic Thinking	Write simple expressions that record calculations with numbers, and interpret numerical expressions without evaluating them.
47	B	Geometry	Understand that attributes belonging to a category of two-dimensional figures also belong to all subcategories of that category.
48	A	Measurement & Data	Convert among different-sized standard measurement units within a given measurement system, and use these conversions in solving multi-step, real world problems.
49	B	Number & Operations-Fractions	Find the area of a rectangle with fractional side lengths by tiling it with unit squares of the appropriate unit fraction side lengths, and show that the area is the same as would be found by multiplying the side lengths. Multiply fractional side lengths to find areas of rectangles, and represent fraction products as rectangular areas.
50	D	Operations/Algebraic Thinking	Write simple expressions that record calculations with numbers, and interpret numerical expressions without evaluating them.

Common Core Mathematics, Practice Test 1, Book 3

Question	Points	Topic	Common Core Skill
51	2	Number & Operations in Base Ten	Perform operations with multi-digit whole numbers. Fluently multiply multi-digit whole numbers using the standard algorithm.
52	2	Operations/Algebraic Thinking	Use parentheses, brackets, or braces in numerical expressions, and evaluate expressions with these symbols.
53	2	Measurement & Data	Convert among different-sized standard measurement units within a given measurement system, and use these conversions in solving multi-step, real world problems.
54	2	Number & Operations-Fractions	Solve word problems involving division of whole numbers leading to answers in the form of fractions or mixed numbers, e.g., by using visual fraction models or equations to represent the problem.
55	2	Number & Operations in Base Ten	Add, subtract, multiply, and divide decimals to hundredths.
56	2	Number & Operations in Base Ten	Add, subtract, multiply, and divide decimals to hundredths.
57	3	Geometry	Represent real world and mathematical problems by graphing points in the first quadrant of the coordinate plane, and interpret coordinate values of points in the context of the situation.
58	3	Measurement & Data	Make a line plot to display a data set of measurements in fractions of a unit (1/2, 1/4, 1/8). Use operations on fractions for this grade to solve problems involving information presented in line plots.
59	3	Number & Operations in Base Ten	Find whole-number quotients of whole numbers with up to four-digit dividends and two-digit divisors, using strategies based on place value, the properties of operations, and/or the relationship between multiplication and division. Illustrate and explain the calculation by using equations, rectangular arrays, and/or area models.
60	3	Number & Operations in Base Ten	Add, subtract, multiply, and divide decimals to hundredths, using concrete models or drawings and strategies based on place value, properties of operations, and/or the relationship between addition and subtraction; relate the strategy to a written method and explain the reasoning used.

Q51.
Answer
33

Work
The work should show the calculation of (48 × 7) – 303 = 33.

Scoring Information
Give a total score of 0, 1, or 2.
Give a score of 1 for the correct answer.
Give a score of 0 or 1 for the working.

Q52.
Answer
34

Work
The work should show the following steps.
$(16 + 20) - 8 \div 4 \rightarrow (36) - 8 \div 4 \rightarrow (36) - 2 \rightarrow 34$

Scoring Information
Give a total score of 0, 1, or 2.
Give a score of 1 for the correct answer.
Give a score of 0 or 1 for the working.

Q53.
Answer
5 pints

Work
The work should show the conversion of 3 quarts to 6 pints, and then the subtraction of 1 pint.

Scoring Information
Give a total score of 0, 1, or 2.
Give a score of 1 for the correct answer.
Give a score of 0 or 1 for the working.

Q54.
Answer
$6\frac{1}{4}$ minutes

Work
The work may show a numerical calculation of 100 ÷ 16, or may use the grid to divide 100 into 16 segments with 4 squares remaining or groups of 16 segments with 4 squares remaining.

Scoring Information
Give a total score of 0, 1, or 2.
Give a score of 1 for the correct answer.
Give a score of 0 or 1 for the working.

Q55.
Answer
973.2 miles

Work
The work should show the calculation of 8192.6 − 7219.4 = 973.2.

Scoring Information
Give a total score of 0, 1, or 2.
Give a score of 1 for the correct answer.
Give a score of 0 or 1 for the working.

Q56.
Answer
$0.55 or 55 cents

Work
The work should show the calculation of (1.85 + 0.95) − 2.25 = 0.55.

Scoring Information
Give a total score of 0, 1, or 2.
Give a score of 1 for the correct answer.
Give a score of 0 or 1 for the working.

Q57.
Answer
(9, 1)

Explanation
The student may describe the calculation (5 + 4, 4 − 3) = (9, 1), or may describe plotting the new point on the grid and reading the coordinates.

Scoring Information
Give a total score of 0, 1, 2, or 3.
Give a score of 1 for the correct answer.
Give a score of 0, 1, or 2 for the explanation.

Q58.
Part A
Answer
The work should show the completed graph as below.

Hailstone Diameter (inches)

```
                X
                X                   X       X
                X       X           X       X       X       X
 ───────────────────────────────────────────────────────────────
     0     1    1    3    1    5    3    7    1
           ─    ─    ─    ─    ─    ─    ─
           8    4    8    2    8    4    8
```

Part B
Answer
$\frac{1}{2}$ inch

Explanation
The student should describe using the line plot to find the middle value.

Scoring Information
Give a total score of 0, 1, 2, or 3.
Give a score of 1 for the correct answer to Part A.
Give a score of 1 for the correct answer to Part B.
Give a score of 0 or 1 for the explanation in Part B.

Q59.
Part A
Answer
$448 = 32h$

Part B
Answer
$14

Work
The work should show solving the equation $448 = 32h$ to find $h = 14$.

Scoring Information
Give a total score of 0, 1, 2, or 3.
Give a score of 1 for the correct answer to Part A.
Give a score of 1 for the correct answer to Part B.
Give a score of 0 or 1 for the working.

Q60.
Answer
0.8 miles

Explanation
The student should describe shading 2.6 on the diagram, shading 1.8 on the diagram, and finding the number of squares shaded only by 2.6. A sample completed diagram is shown below.

Scoring Information
Give a total score of 0, 1, 2, or 3.
Give a score of 1 for the correct answer.
Give a score of 0, 1, or 2 for the explanation.

Common Core Mathematics, Practice Test 2, Book 1

Question	Answer	Topic	Common Core Skill
1	B	Number & Operations in Base Ten	Add, subtract, multiply, and divide decimals to hundredths, using concrete models or drawings.
2	D	Number & Operations-Fractions	Interpret division of a whole number by a unit fraction, and compute such quotients.
3	A	Number & Operations-Fractions	Add and subtract fractions with unlike denominators (including mixed numbers).
4	C	Geometry	Classify two-dimensional figures in a hierarchy based on properties.
5	B	Number & Operations in Base Ten	Fluently multiply multi-digit whole numbers using the standard algorithm.
6	C	Number & Operations-Fractions	Interpret division of a unit fraction by a non-zero whole number, and compute such quotients.
7	D	Operations/Algebraic Thinking	Use parentheses, brackets, or braces in numerical expressions, and evaluate expressions with these symbols.
8	B	Measurement & Data	Convert among different-sized standard measurement units within a given measurement system, and use these conversions in solving multi-step, real world problems.
9	C	Number & Operations-Fractions	Interpret a fraction as division of the numerator by the denominator.
10	D	Number & Operations-Fractions	Solve word problems involving addition and subtraction of fractions referring to the same whole, including cases of unlike denominators, e.g., by using visual fraction models or equations to represent the problem.
11	D	Number & Operations in Base Ten	Fluently multiply multi-digit whole numbers using the standard algorithm.
12	C	Number & Operations-Fractions	Interpret a fraction as division of the numerator by the denominator.
13	B	Measurement & Data	Convert among different-sized standard measurement units within a given measurement system, and use these conversions in solving multi-step, real world problems.
14	C	Operations/Algebraic Thinking	Analyze patterns and relationships by identifying apparent relationships between corresponding terms.
15	D	Number & Operations in Base Ten	Find whole-number quotients of whole numbers with up to four-digit dividends and two-digit divisors, using strategies based on properties of operations.
16	A	Geometry	Classify two-dimensional figures in a hierarchy based on properties.
17	D	Geometry	Locate a point in a coordinate system by using an ordered pair of numbers, called its coordinates.
18	B	Operations/Algebraic Thinking	Analyze patterns and relationships by identifying apparent relationships between corresponding terms.

19	C	Measurement & Data	Recognize volume as an attribute of solid figures and understand concepts of volume measurement.
20	D	Geometry	Classify two-dimensional figures in a hierarchy based on properties.
21	C	Operations/Algebraic Thinking	Use parentheses, brackets, or braces in numerical expressions, and evaluate expressions with these symbols.
22	B	Operations/Algebraic Thinking	Write simple expressions that record calculations with numbers, and interpret numerical expressions without evaluating them.
23	B	Geometry	Use a coordinate system and understand that the first number indicates how far to travel from the origin in the direction of one axis, and the second number indicates how far to travel in the direction of the second axis.
24	B	Number & Operations in Base Ten	Explain patterns in the placement of the decimal point when a decimal is multiplied or divided by a power of 10.
25	D	Number & Operations in Base Ten	Read and write decimals to thousandths using base-ten numerals, number names, and expanded form.

Common Core Mathematics, Practice Test 2, Book 2

Question	Answer	Topic	Common Core Skill
26	A	Geometry	Classify two-dimensional figures in a hierarchy based on properties.
27	C	Operations/Algebraic Thinking	Analyze patterns and relationships by identifying apparent relationships between corresponding terms.
28	D	Operations/Algebraic Thinking	Write simple expressions that record calculations with numbers, and interpret numerical expressions without evaluating them.
29	A	Number & Operations in Base Ten	Use place value understanding to round decimals to any place.
30	C	Operations/Algebraic Thinking	Use parentheses, brackets, or braces in numerical expressions, and evaluate expressions with these symbols.
31	B	Operations/Algebraic Thinking	Analyze patterns and relationships by identifying apparent relationships between corresponding terms.
32	A	Number & Operations in Base Ten	Find whole-number quotients of whole numbers with up to four-digit dividends and two-digit divisors, using strategies based on place value, the properties of operations, and/or the relationship between multiplication and division.
33	D	Number & Operations in Base Ten	Compare two decimals to thousandths based on meanings of the digits in each place, using >, =, and < symbols to record the results of comparisons.
34	D	Number & Operations-Fractions	Solve real world problems involving multiplication of fractions and mixed numbers.
35	C	Operations/Algebraic Thinking	Analyze patterns and relationships by identifying apparent relationships between corresponding terms.
36	B	Number & Operations in Base Ten	Compare two decimals to thousandths based on meanings of the digits in each place, using >, =, and < symbols to record the results of comparisons.
37	A	Number & Operations in Base Ten	Find whole-number quotients of whole numbers with up to four-digit dividends and two-digit divisors, using strategies based on the relationship between multiplication and division.
38	A	Number & Operations in Base Ten	Illustrate and explain calculations by using equations, rectangular arrays, and/or area models.
39	D	Number & Operations in Base Ten	Explain patterns in the placement of the decimal point when a decimal is multiplied or divided by a power of 10.
40	D	Geometry	Understand that attributes belonging to a category of two-dimensional figures also belong to all subcategories of that category.
41	A	Number & Operations-Fractions	Explaining why multiplying a given number by a fraction greater than 1 results in a product greater than the given number.
42	C	Operations/Algebraic Thinking	Generate two numerical patterns using two given rules. Identify apparent relationships between corresponding terms.

43	D	Number & Operations in Base Ten	Perform operations with multi-digit whole numbers.
44	B	Number & Operations in Base Ten	Perform operations with multi-digit whole numbers.
45	D	Number & Operations in Base Ten	Find whole-number quotients of whole numbers. Illustrate and explain the calculation by using equations, rectangular arrays, and/or area models.
46	D	Operations/Algebraic Thinking	Write simple expressions that record calculations with numbers, and interpret numerical expressions without evaluating them.
47	B	Operations/Algebraic Thinking	Analyze patterns and relationships by identifying apparent relationships between corresponding terms.
48	A	Geometry	Classify two-dimensional figures in a hierarchy based on properties.
49	B	Number & Operations in Base Ten	Recognize that in a multi-digit number, a digit in one place represents 10 times as much as it represents in the place to its right and 1/10 of what it represents in the place to its left.
50	C	Number & Operations-Fractions	Interpret multiplication as scaling (resizing) by comparing the size of a product to the size of one factor on the basis of the size of the other factor, without performing the indicated multiplication.

Common Core Mathematics, Practice Test 2, Book 3

Question	Points	Topic	Common Core Skill
51	2	Number & Operations in Base Ten	Find whole-number quotients of whole numbers with up to four-digit dividends and two-digit divisors, using strategies based on place value, the properties of operations, and/or the relationship between multiplication and division.
52	2	Number & Operations in Base Ten	Add, subtract, multiply, and divide decimals to hundredths.
53	2	Geometry	Locate a point in a coordinate system by using an ordered pair of numbers, called its coordinates. Understand the convention that the names of the two axes and the coordinates correspond (e.g., x-axis and x-coordinate, y-axis and y-coordinate).
54	2	Measurement & Data	Measure volumes by counting unit cubes, using cubic cm, cubic in, cubic ft, and improvised units.
55	2	Number & Operations-Fractions	Find the area of a rectangle with fractional side lengths by tiling it with unit squares of the appropriate unit fraction side lengths, and show that the area is the same as would be found by multiplying the side lengths. Multiply fractional side lengths to find areas of rectangles, and represent fraction products as rectangular areas.
56	2	Number & Operations-Fractions	Apply and extend previous understandings of multiplication to multiply a fraction or whole number by a fraction.
57	3	Geometry	Represent real world and mathematical problems by graphing points in the first quadrant of the coordinate plane, and interpret coordinate values of points in the context of the situation.
58	3	Geometry	Understand that attributes belonging to a category of two-dimensional figures also belong to all subcategories of that category.
59	3	Geometry	Classify two-dimensional figures in a hierarchy based on properties.
60	3	Number & Operations-Fractions	Solve word problems involving addition and subtraction of fractions referring to the same whole, including cases of unlike denominators. Apply and extend previous understandings of multiplication to multiply a fraction or whole number by a fraction.

Q51.
Answer
16

Work
The work may show the calculation of 192 ÷ 12 = 16. The work could also show a diagram representing 16 rows of 12.

Scoring Information
Give a total score of 0, 1, or 2.
Give a score of 1 for the correct answer.
Give a score of 0 or 1 for the working.

Q52.
Answer
$2.60

Work
The work could show the calculation of 20 – (14.85 + 2.55) = 2.60 or could show the two-step subtraction of 20 – 14.85 = 5.15 and 5.15 – 2.55 = 2.60.

Scoring Information
Give a total score of 0, 1, or 2.
Give a score of 1 for the correct answer.
Give a score of 0 or 1 for the working.

Q53.
Part A
Answer
The student should complete the table as shown below.

x	0	2	4
y	8	5	2

Part B
Answer
(0, 8)

Scoring Information
Give a total score of 0, 1, or 2.
Give a score of 1 for the correct answer to Part A.
Give a score of 1 for the correct answer to Part B.

Q54.

Answer

24 cubic inches or 24 in^3

Work

The work may show the calculation of $8 \times 3 \times 1 = 24$ or could show that the student counted the cubes.

Scoring Information

Give a total score of 0, 1, or 2.
Give a score of 1 for the correct numerical answer.
Give a score of 1 for the correct units.

Q55.

Answer

$\frac{9}{16}$ square feet

Work

The diagram should be shaded to show a 3×3 section, as shown. The student should recognize that 9 out of 16 squares are shaded, so the area is $\frac{9}{16}$ square feet.

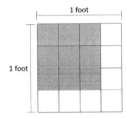

Scoring Information

Give a total score of 0, 1, or 2.
Give a score of 1 for the correct answer.
Give a score of 0 or 1 for the working.

Q56.
Answer

$\dfrac{1}{3}$

Work

The student may find the area painted on the two days as $\dfrac{1}{2}$ and $\dfrac{1}{2} \times \dfrac{1}{3} = \dfrac{1}{6}$, and then find the remaining area by calculating $1 - \dfrac{1}{2} - \dfrac{1}{6} = \dfrac{2}{3}$. The student may also use a diagram such as the one below to find the area remaining.

Day 1	Day 1	Day 1
Day 2	Day 3	Day 3

Scoring Information
Give a total score of 0, 1, or 2.
Give a score of 1 for the correct answer.
Give a score of 0 or 1 for the working.

Q57.
Answer
(8, 8)

Explanation

The student may describe the calculation (6 + 2, 5 + 3) = (8, 8), or may describe plotting the new point on the grid and reading the coordinates.

Scoring Information
Give a total score of 0, 1, 2, or 3.
Give a score of 1 for the correct answer.
Give a score of 0, 1, or 2 for the explanation.

Q58.
Part A
Answer
BA and CD, BC and AD

Part B
The student should identify that the shape is a rhombus. The explanation should refer to the two pairs of parallel sides and the four sides being equal in length. The explanation may also include that the shape is not a square because the angles are not right angles.

Scoring Information
Give a total score of 0, 1, 2, or 3.
Give a score of 1 for the correct answer to Part A.
Give a score of 1 for the correct shape identified in Part B.
Give a score of 0 or 1 for the explanation in Part B.

Q59.
Part A
Answer
The student should circle the following statement.
At least 1 pair of parallel sides

Part B
Answer
The student should identify that 4 congruent sides could be used to tell the difference between a rectangle and a square. The answer should show an understanding that all the statements are true for both rectangles and squares except that a square has 4 congruent sides and a rectangle does not.

Scoring Information
Give a total score of 0, 1, 2, or 3.
Give a score of 1 for the correct statement circled in Part A.
Give a score of 1 for identifying the correct statement in Part B.
Give a score of 0 or 1 for the explanation in Part B.

Q60.
Part A
Answer
$\dfrac{7}{24}$

Work
The student may add the three fractions to find $\dfrac{17}{24}$ and then calculate $1 - \dfrac{17}{24} = \dfrac{7}{24}$.
The student may convert all the fractions to those with denominators of 24, and then calculate $\dfrac{24}{24} - \dfrac{6}{24} - \dfrac{9}{24} - \dfrac{2}{24} = \dfrac{7}{24}$.
The student could also use a diagram to find the remaining fraction, such as the one below.

Pumpkin	Pumpkin	Pumpkin	Apple	Apple	Apple
Pumpkin	Pumpkin	Pumpkin	Apple	Apple	Apple
Pumpkin	Pumpkin	Pumpkin	**Peach**	**Peach**	**Peach**
Cherry	Cherry	**Peach**	**Peach**	**Peach**	**Peach**

Part B
Answer
30

Work
The work should show the calculation of $360 \times \dfrac{1}{12} = 30$. The work could show an understanding that $360 \times \dfrac{1}{12}$ is the same as $\dfrac{360}{12}$ or $360 \div 12$.

Scoring Information
Give a total score of 0, 1, 2, or 3.
Give a score of 1 for the correct answer to Part A.
Give a score of 1 for the correct answer to Part B.
Give a score of 0 or 1 for the working.

Answer Sheet: Practice Test 1

	Book 1				Book 2			
1	Ⓐ Ⓑ Ⓒ Ⓓ	**16**	Ⓐ Ⓑ Ⓒ Ⓓ	**26**	Ⓐ Ⓑ Ⓒ Ⓓ	**41**	Ⓐ Ⓑ Ⓒ Ⓓ
2	Ⓐ Ⓑ Ⓒ Ⓓ	**17**	Ⓐ Ⓑ Ⓒ Ⓓ	**27**	Ⓐ Ⓑ Ⓒ Ⓓ	**42**	Ⓐ Ⓑ Ⓒ Ⓓ
3	Ⓐ Ⓑ Ⓒ Ⓓ	**18**	Ⓐ Ⓑ Ⓒ Ⓓ	**28**	Ⓐ Ⓑ Ⓒ Ⓓ	**43**	Ⓐ Ⓑ Ⓒ Ⓓ
4	Ⓐ Ⓑ Ⓒ Ⓓ	**19**	Ⓐ Ⓑ Ⓒ Ⓓ	**29**	Ⓐ Ⓑ Ⓒ Ⓓ	**44**	Ⓐ Ⓑ Ⓒ Ⓓ
5	Ⓐ Ⓑ Ⓒ Ⓓ	**20**	Ⓐ Ⓑ Ⓒ Ⓓ	**30**	Ⓐ Ⓑ Ⓒ Ⓓ	**45**	Ⓐ Ⓑ Ⓒ Ⓓ
6	Ⓐ Ⓑ Ⓒ Ⓓ	**21**	Ⓐ Ⓑ Ⓒ Ⓓ	**31**	Ⓐ Ⓑ Ⓒ Ⓓ	**46**	Ⓐ Ⓑ Ⓒ Ⓓ
7	Ⓐ Ⓑ Ⓒ Ⓓ	**22**	Ⓐ Ⓑ Ⓒ Ⓓ	**32**	Ⓐ Ⓑ Ⓒ Ⓓ	**47**	Ⓐ Ⓑ Ⓒ Ⓓ
8	Ⓐ Ⓑ Ⓒ Ⓓ	**23**	Ⓐ Ⓑ Ⓒ Ⓓ	**33**	Ⓐ Ⓑ Ⓒ Ⓓ	**48**	Ⓐ Ⓑ Ⓒ Ⓓ
9	Ⓐ Ⓑ Ⓒ Ⓓ	**24**	Ⓐ Ⓑ Ⓒ Ⓓ	**34**	Ⓐ Ⓑ Ⓒ Ⓓ	**49**	Ⓐ Ⓑ Ⓒ Ⓓ
10	Ⓐ Ⓑ Ⓒ Ⓓ	**25**	Ⓐ Ⓑ Ⓒ Ⓓ	**35**	Ⓐ Ⓑ Ⓒ Ⓓ	**50**	Ⓐ Ⓑ Ⓒ Ⓓ
11	Ⓐ Ⓑ Ⓒ Ⓓ			**36**	Ⓐ Ⓑ Ⓒ Ⓓ		
12	Ⓐ Ⓑ Ⓒ Ⓓ			**37**	Ⓐ Ⓑ Ⓒ Ⓓ		
13	Ⓐ Ⓑ Ⓒ Ⓓ			**38**	Ⓐ Ⓑ Ⓒ Ⓓ		
14	Ⓐ Ⓑ Ⓒ Ⓓ			**39**	Ⓐ Ⓑ Ⓒ Ⓓ		
15	Ⓐ Ⓑ Ⓒ Ⓓ			**40**	Ⓐ Ⓑ Ⓒ Ⓓ		

Book 3

Write the answers to the questions in Book 3 in your test book.

Answer Sheet: Practice Test 2

Book 1				Book 2			
1	Ⓐ Ⓑ Ⓒ Ⓓ	16	Ⓐ Ⓑ Ⓒ Ⓓ	26	Ⓐ Ⓑ Ⓒ Ⓓ	41	Ⓐ Ⓑ Ⓒ Ⓓ
2	Ⓐ Ⓑ Ⓒ Ⓓ	17	Ⓐ Ⓑ Ⓒ Ⓓ	27	Ⓐ Ⓑ Ⓒ Ⓓ	42	Ⓐ Ⓑ Ⓒ Ⓓ
3	Ⓐ Ⓑ Ⓒ Ⓓ	18	Ⓐ Ⓑ Ⓒ Ⓓ	28	Ⓐ Ⓑ Ⓒ Ⓓ	43	Ⓐ Ⓑ Ⓒ Ⓓ
4	Ⓐ Ⓑ Ⓒ Ⓓ	19	Ⓐ Ⓑ Ⓒ Ⓓ	29	Ⓐ Ⓑ Ⓒ Ⓓ	44	Ⓐ Ⓑ Ⓒ Ⓓ
5	Ⓐ Ⓑ Ⓒ Ⓓ	20	Ⓐ Ⓑ Ⓒ Ⓓ	30	Ⓐ Ⓑ Ⓒ Ⓓ	45	Ⓐ Ⓑ Ⓒ Ⓓ
6	Ⓐ Ⓑ Ⓒ Ⓓ	21	Ⓐ Ⓑ Ⓒ Ⓓ	31	Ⓐ Ⓑ Ⓒ Ⓓ	46	Ⓐ Ⓑ Ⓒ Ⓓ
7	Ⓐ Ⓑ Ⓒ Ⓓ	22	Ⓐ Ⓑ Ⓒ Ⓓ	32	Ⓐ Ⓑ Ⓒ Ⓓ	47	Ⓐ Ⓑ Ⓒ Ⓓ
8	Ⓐ Ⓑ Ⓒ Ⓓ	23	Ⓐ Ⓑ Ⓒ Ⓓ	33	Ⓐ Ⓑ Ⓒ Ⓓ	48	Ⓐ Ⓑ Ⓒ Ⓓ
9	Ⓐ Ⓑ Ⓒ Ⓓ	24	Ⓐ Ⓑ Ⓒ Ⓓ	34	Ⓐ Ⓑ Ⓒ Ⓓ	49	Ⓐ Ⓑ Ⓒ Ⓓ
10	Ⓐ Ⓑ Ⓒ Ⓓ	25	Ⓐ Ⓑ Ⓒ Ⓓ	35	Ⓐ Ⓑ Ⓒ Ⓓ	50	Ⓐ Ⓑ Ⓒ Ⓓ
11	Ⓐ Ⓑ Ⓒ Ⓓ			36	Ⓐ Ⓑ Ⓒ Ⓓ		
12	Ⓐ Ⓑ Ⓒ Ⓓ			37	Ⓐ Ⓑ Ⓒ Ⓓ		
13	Ⓐ Ⓑ Ⓒ Ⓓ			38	Ⓐ Ⓑ Ⓒ Ⓓ		
14	Ⓐ Ⓑ Ⓒ Ⓓ			39	Ⓐ Ⓑ Ⓒ Ⓓ		
15	Ⓐ Ⓑ Ⓒ Ⓓ			40	Ⓐ Ⓑ Ⓒ Ⓓ		

Book 3

Write the answers to the questions in Book 3 in your test book.

Made in the USA
Middletown, DE
23 June 2015